ADRIAN LIBRARY

Many Cultures, One World

Pakistan

by Gina DeAngelis

Consultant:
Keith Snodgrass
Associate Director and Outreach Coordinator
　for South Asia Center
Jackson School of International Studies
University of Washington, Seattle

Blue Earth Books

an imprint of Capstone Press
Mankato, Minnesota

Blue Earth Books are published by Capstone Press
151 Good Counsel Drive, P.O. Box 669, Mankato, Minnesota 56002
http://www.capstone-press.com

Copyright © 2004 by Capstone Press. All rights reserved.

No part of this book may be reproduced in whole or in part, or stored in a retrieval system, or transmitted in any form or by any means, electronic, mechanical, photocopying, recording, or otherwise, without written permission from the publisher. For information regarding permission, write to Capstone Press, 151 Good Counsel Drive, P.O. Box 669, Dept. R, Mankato, Minnesota 56002.
Printed in the United States of America

Library of Congress Cataloging-in-Publication Data
DeAngelis, Gina.
  Pakistan / by Gina DeAngelis.
     v. cm.—(Many cultures, one world)
  Contents: Welcome to Pakistan—A Pakistani legend—City and country life—Seasons in Pakistan—Family life in Pakistan—Laws, rules, and customs—Pets in Pakistan—Sites to see in Pakistan.
  Includes bibliographical references and index.
  ISBN 0-7368-2169-4 (hardcover)
  1. Pakistan—Juvenile literature. [1. Pakistan.] I. Title. II. Series.
DS376.9.D46 2004
954.91—dc21   2002155269

Summary: An introduction to the geography, culture, and people of Pakistan, including a map, legend, recipe, craft, and game.

Editorial credits
Editor: Katy Kudela
Series Designer: Kia Adams
Photo Researcher: Alta Schaffer
Product Planning Editor: Karen Risch

Cover photo of farm couple harvesting wheat, by Corbis/Jonathan Blair

Artistic effects
Brand X Pictures/PictureQuest

Photo credits
The British Library/Image Works, 11
Bruce Coleman Inc., 27 (right)
Capstone Press/Gary Sundermeyer, 3 (top right, bottom left), 19, 25
Corbis/Galen Rowell, 17 (right); Brian A. Vikander, 18
Cory Langley, 20-21
Eileen R. Herrling, 4-5, 21 (right)
Hahn/Laif/Aurora, 22-23, 24
Joe Viesti / The Viesti Collection Inc., 6, 16-17, 29 (right)
Markus Kirchgessner/Bilderberg/Aurora, 12-13, 15, 26-27
One Mile Up Inc., 23 (top)
Provided by Audrius Tomonis-www.banknotes.com, 23 (bottom)
SuperStock/Hubertus Kanus, 8-9
TRIP, 10; W. Jacobs, 13 (right); Tibor Bognar, 14; B. Brawshaw, 28-29

1 2 3 4 5 6 08 07 06 05 04 03

Contents

Chapter 1
Welcome to Pakistan 4

Chapter 2
A Pakistani Legend 8

Chapter 3
City and Country Life 12

Chapter 4
Seasons in Pakistan 16

Chapter 5
Family Life in Pakistan 20

Chapter 6
Laws, Rules, and Customs 22

Chapter 7
Pets in Pakistan 26

Chapter 8
Sites to See in Pakistan 28

Words to Know 30
To Learn More 30
Useful Addresses 31
Internet Sites 31
Index 32

Check out page 7 to find a map of Pakistan.

See page 15 to learn how to play a favorite game of Pakistani children.

Turn to page 19 to find out how to make a yogurt drink.

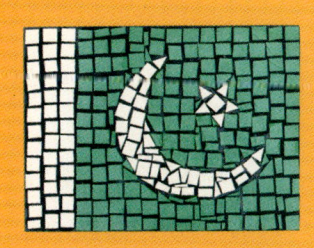

Look at page 25 to learn how to make a mosaic of Pakistan's flag.

CHAPTER 1

Welcome to Pakistan

Towering mountains stretch across northern Pakistan in southern Asia. Three great mountain ranges come together here. They are the Karakoram, Himalaya, and Hindu Kush.

The second tallest mountain in the world is found in the Karakoram Range. It is called K2. In 1856, British Colonel T. G. Montgomery measured the range. He named the Karakoram mountain peaks in the order he saw them. Today, K2 is still known by the name Montgomery first gave to it.

Tall mountains stretch across northern Pakistan.

Facts about Pakistan

Name: ....Islamic Republic of Pakistan
Capital: ....Islamabad
Population: ....130 million people
Size: ....307,374 square miles
.........................(796,099 square kilometers)
Languages: ....Urdu, Punjabi, Sindhi, Pashtu,
.........................Balochi, Siraiki, Hindko, Brahui
Religion: ....Islam
Highest point: ...K2, 28,251 feet (8,611 meters)
.........................above sea level
Lowest point: ....Arabian Sea, sea level
Main crops: ....Cotton, rice
Money: ....Pakistani rupee

Pakistan is a long, narrow country. It is about the size of California, Oregon, and Washington combined. But about three times as many people live in Pakistan as in these three U.S. states.

Pakistan's land is divided into four areas. The plains of Sindh hold cotton, fruit, wheat, rice, and sugar farms. The crowded Punjab area has many farms and factories. The Baluchistan area is the largest but has the fewest people. The North-West Frontier Province (NWFP) has farms, orchards, and high mountains. Many people from Afghanistan now live in the NWFP.

Some people in Pakistan's cities travel by horse-drawn buggies called tongas.

Map of Pakistan

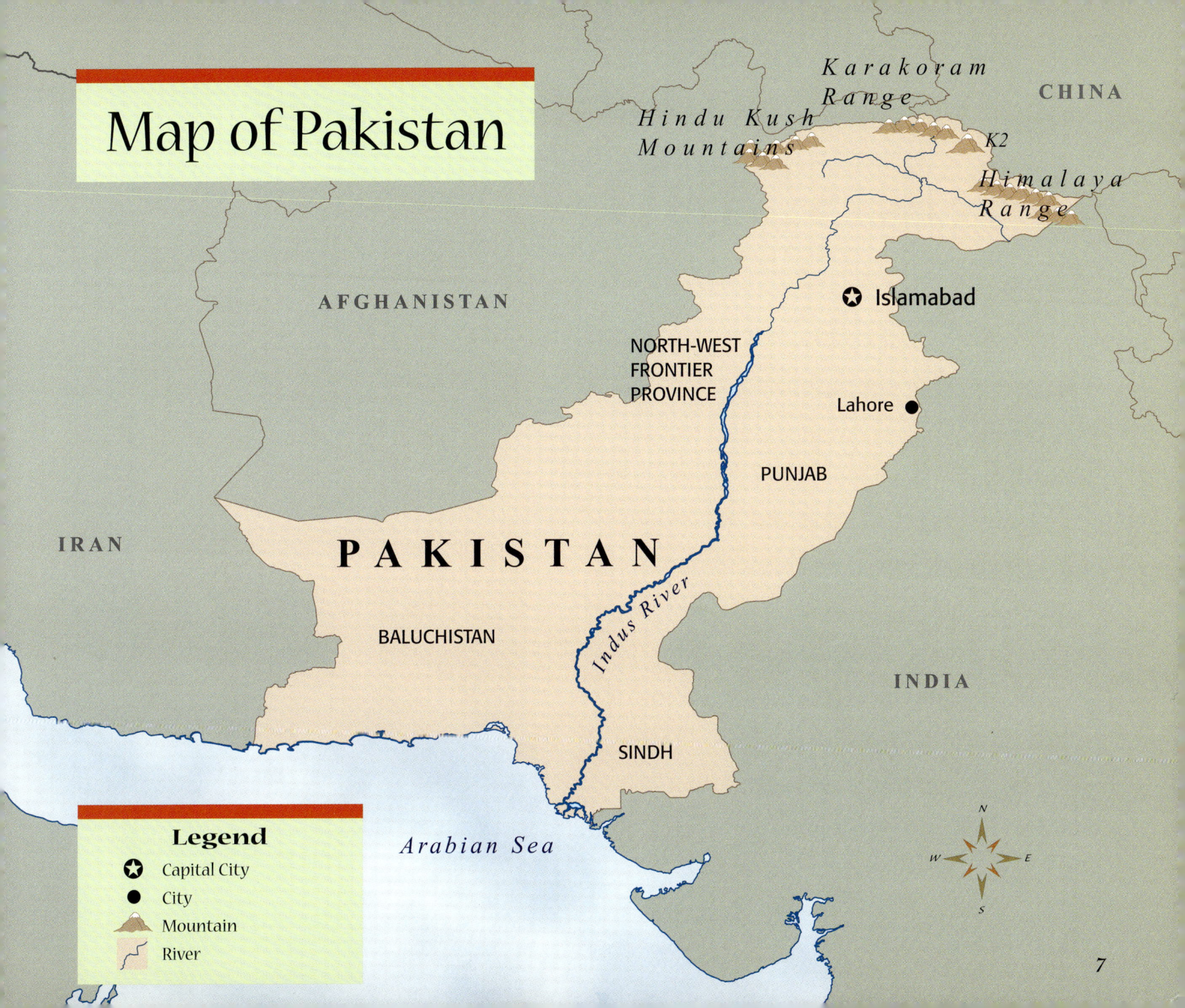

Legend
- ⍟ Capital City
- ● City
- ⛰ Mountain
- ~ River

CHAPTER 2

A Pakistani Legend

Pakistani people have told stories for thousands of years. Parents told stories to their children. Each storyteller added interesting details to make the story more exciting. These stories often combined truth with make-believe. Most legends are based on fact, but they are not entirely true.

Legends sometimes combine customs of different people. Since Pakistan and India are close neighbors, their people share a history. They also share the legend of Sohni and Mahiwal.

Storytellers pass on interesting stories. One Pakistani story tells of a cat that wanted a fish but did not want to get its paws wet.

The Legend of Sohni and Mahiwal

The land of Pakistan was once known as Gujrat. The land was filled with many small villages. A master potter named Tulla lived in Gujrat. He made pots so beautiful that everyone north of India wanted them. Many traders came to buy Tulla's pots.

One day a trader named Izzat Beg came to Gujrat. He planned to buy a bowl or a jar in Tulla's shop. In a corner of the shop, Beg saw Tulla's daughter, Sohni. She was painting designs on a pot. When Beg and Sohni saw each other, they fell in love.

Tulla did not believe Beg was the right husband for Sohni. Tulla decided his daughter should marry someone else. The Gujrat custom was for a father to arrange his daughter's marriage. Sohni wanted to be with Beg. But she had to obey her father's wishes.

Soon, Sohni began her new life as a wife. She lived with her husband in the next village. But Sohni could not forget Beg, and he could not forget her.

Beg began living in a small hut across the river from Sohni's new home. He earned his living

Tulla was the name of the potter in the story. Today, many Pakistani artists still make colorful pottery.

tending other people's cattle and buffalo. People in the village began to call him Mahiwal, a name that means "cowherd."

Sohni and Mahiwal's love was so great that they met every night. Mahiwal swam across the river to be with Sohni. They kept their meetings secret for quite some time. But one day, Mahiwal hurt his leg. He was no longer strong enough to swim across the river.

The next night, Sohni decided to swim across the river to Mahiwal. She was not a strong swimmer, so she held a covered pottery jar in her arms. The empty jar helped Sohni stay afloat. Night after night, Sohni floated across the river to Mahiwal's hut.

Everyone in the village had been talking about Sohni and Mahiwal. One night, Sohni's sister-in-law saw her leave with the pottery jar. The sister-in-law was angry. She thought it was unfair that her brother's wife loved another man. She decided to put an end to Sohni and Mahiwal's secret meetings.

The next night, the sister-in-law put an unbaked pottery jar in place of the hard-baked one. Sohni did not notice the difference. When Sohni tried to cross the river, the water made the unbaked pottery jar crumble into pieces.

As Mahiwal watched, Sohni sank beneath the water. He jumped in to save her, but he could not swim with his injured leg. Both Sohni and Mahiwal drowned. The next day, their bodies were found washed up side-by-side on the shore of the river.

A river separated Sohni and Mahiwal. But they found a way to cross the river to see each other.

CHAPTER 3

City and Country Life

People in Pakistan's cities often work in factories or as crafters. Factory workers make textiles, bricks, fertilizers, leather, and cement. Crafters sell their carpets, blankets, pottery, brass work, and woodcarvings.

In cities, Pakistanis live in crowded neighborhoods. Many people live in apartments. Others have small houses built close together. A few Pakistanis live in larger, more modern houses.

Most people in Pakistan live in the country. They work as farmers or herders.

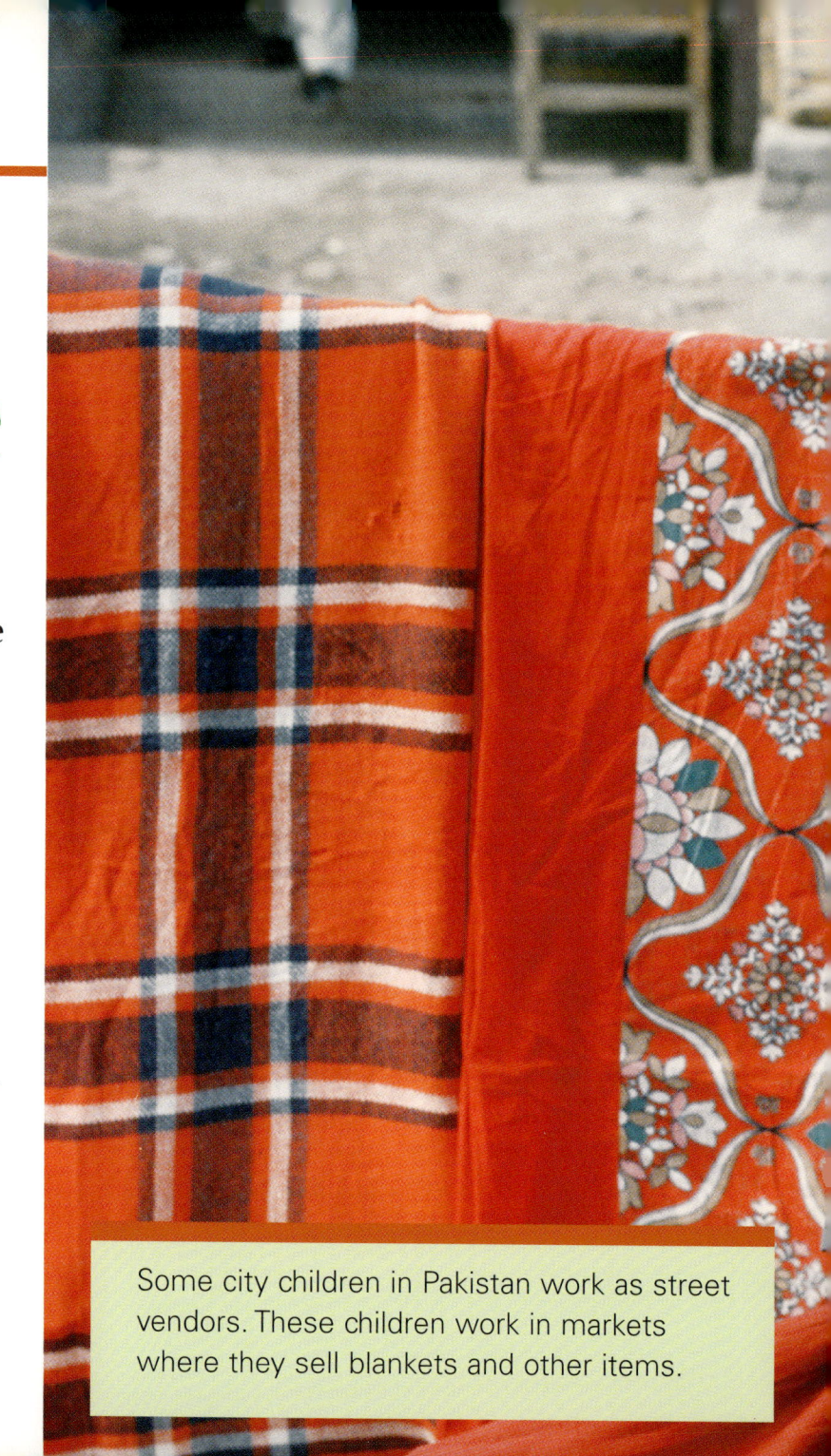

Some city children in Pakistan work as street vendors. These children work in markets where they sell blankets and other items.

Many Pakistanis live in the country and work as farmers.

Many farmers grow rice and cotton. Some raise cattle and water buffalo. Herders keep sheep, goats, and camels.

Homes in rural Pakistan are simple. Houses have two or three rooms with little furniture. Homes in the country usually do not have electricity or running water. Many people carry their water from a village well.

Walking is the most common form of transportation in Pakistan. Few people own cars. People also travel by city buses, public vans, and taxicabs.

Pakistanis use special transportation for long trips. Many people going long distances travel in beautifully decorated buses and trucks. A few Pakistani cities have railroads and airports.

Many people travel by colorful trucks or buses during long trips across the country.

Clap, Clap, Snap, Snap

Schoolchildren in Pakistan enjoy playing the popular game "Clap, Clap, Snap, Snap." Children in Pakistan might also play a word game like this one on a long trip.

What You Need
four to eight players

What You Do
1. Players stand in a circle.
2. Choose a player to start the game.
3. A player starts the game by shouting out a topic. Ideas for topics include country names, colors, and flowers.
4. Each player in the circle tries to give a different answer. Answers should go around the circle clock-wise.
5. While a player is thinking of an answer, the other players should clap twice and snap their fingers twice to keep rhythm. This is the amount of time each player has to give an answer.
6. Players who fail to answer in this amount of time are out of the game.
7. The topic must go around the circle for two rounds before it can change. Players can take turns choosing topics for the game.
8. The player who stays in the circle the longest is the winner.

CHAPTER 4

Seasons in Pakistan

Pakistan has three seasons. The hot season begins in March and ends in June. The cold season runs from October through February. The wet season starts in July and goes through September.

Pakistan has very hot and very cold temperatures. In the hot season, temperatures can reach 122 degrees Fahrenheit (50 degrees Celsius). In the cold season, temperatures can dip to minus 36 degrees Fahrenheit (minus 38 degrees Celsius).

People in Pakistan travel through the desert on camels. Camels do well in the hot temperatures.

People who hike through Pakistan's mountains must dress warmly for cooler temperatures. Snow covers many of Pakistan's mountains all year.

Pakistan's wet season usually is not very wet. Large areas of the country get little rain. Only about one-fourth of Pakistan gets more than 10 inches (25 centimeters) of rain each year. But sometimes there are floods during Pakistan's wet season.

Much of the farmland in Pakistan must be watered, or irrigated, to make anything grow. People in Pakistan rely on the Indus River for water. The Indus stretches 1,690 miles (2,720 kilometers). It is the longest river in Pakistan.

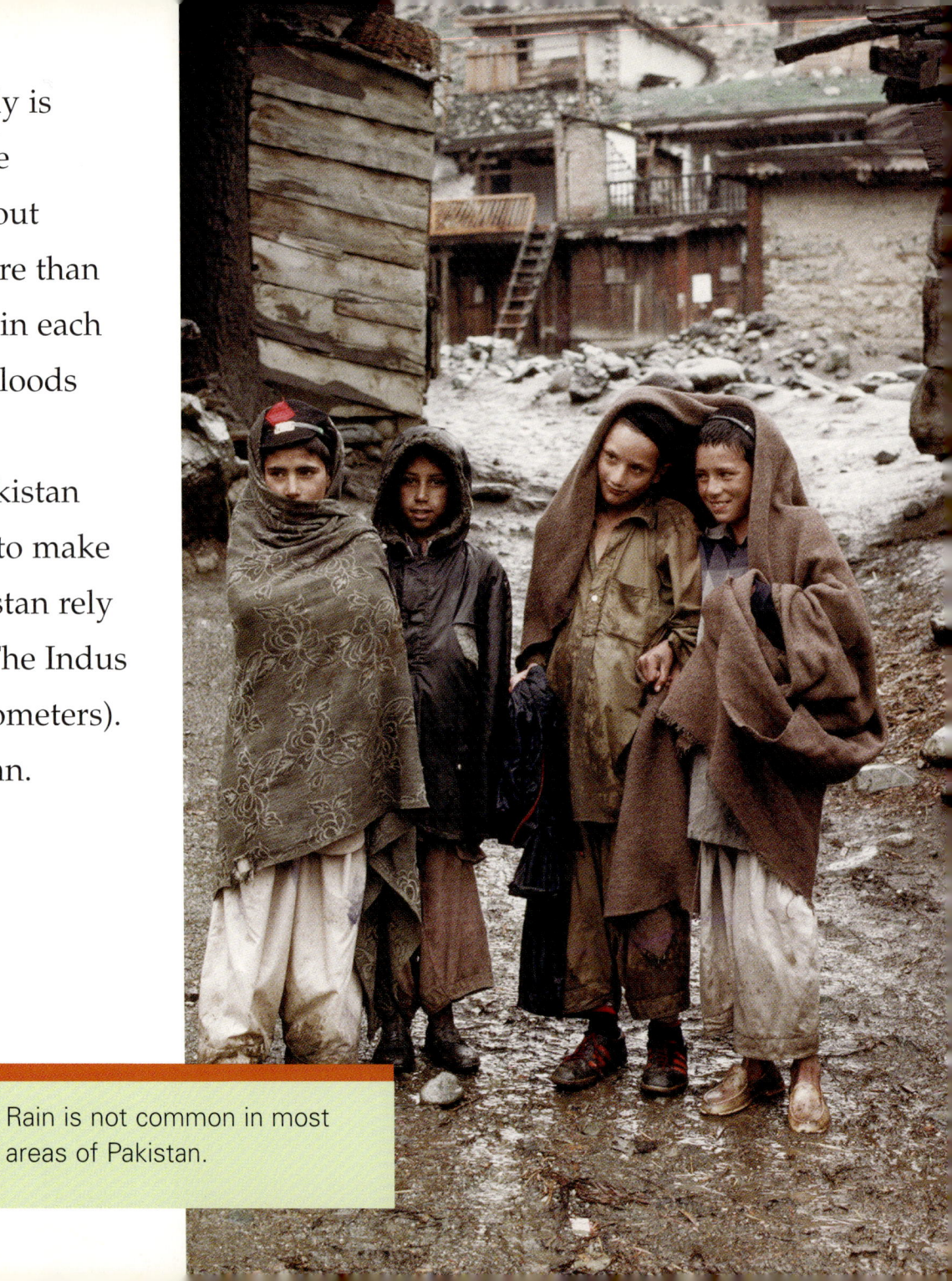

Rain is not common in most areas of Pakistan.

Lassi

People in Pakistan use yogurt in many different recipes. On hot days, many people in Pakistan enjoy a yogurt drink called lassi.

What You Need

Ingredients
1 cup (240 mL) plain yogurt
1 cup (240 mL) cold water
1 tablespoon (15 mL) honey
1 cup (240 mL) crushed ice
1 teaspoon (5 mL) cinnamon
1 banana

Equipment
dry-ingredient measuring cup
measuring spoons
electric blender
2 medium drinking glasses

What You Do

1. Put all the ingredients in an electric blender.
2. With an adult's help, blend ingredients well.
3. Pour mixture into drinking glasses.
4. Sprinkle cinnamon on top.
5. Serve drinks immediately.

Makes about 2 servings

CHAPTER 5

Family Life in Pakistan

In many areas, Pakistani families are very poor. Parents and children must work to help the family survive. Farm children often help in the fields. City children work in factories or hold other jobs.

Most Pakistani homes are small and crowded. Several generations of a Pakistani family share the same house. It is common for children, parents, grandparents, and even great-grandparents to live together. But even the smallest houses have a separate room or cot for guests.

Many Pakistani families live in rural villages.

Birthdays in Pakistan

City children in Pakistan celebrate birthdays much like children in the United States do. Most parties include a cake, balloons, and party hats. Sometimes parents take children to the nearest zoo or park to celebrate a birthday.

Children in rural areas of Pakistan often do not celebrate their birthdays. Rural children are often born at home. Sometimes parents do not keep track of the exact dates of their children's birthdays. When rural children do celebrate their birthdays, they usually receive a few coins to buy toffee candies or cookies.

CHAPTER 6

Laws, Rules, and Customs

Islam is the official religion of Pakistan. Most Pakistanis are Muslim. They follow the teachings of a holy book called the Qur'an. The Islamic faith has many rules. Faithful Muslims follow these rules. They pray five times a day and do not eat pork.

No matter how small, every Pakistani village has a holy building called a mosque. Mosques usually have domes at the top. They also have towers called minarets.

Pakistan's national flag is dark green and white. A white column appears on the left side of the flag. The green represents Islam. The white represents other religions. A white crescent and star sit in the center of the flag. The crescent stands for progress. The star represents knowledge.

Pakistan's flag was adopted in 1947 when Pakistan became a nation. Muhammad Ali Jinnah designed Pakistan's flag.

Pakistan's money is called the rupee. One Pakistani rupee equals 100 paisas. Rupees come in paper bills and coins.

23

Most special days in Pakistan are religious holidays. Ramadan is the ninth month of the Muslim year. During this month, Muslims do not eat or drink from sunrise to sundown. After the month of fasting, Muslims celebrate the end of Ramadan. Eid-al-Fitr, or Small Eid, is a special feast.

Pakistani children are not required to go to school. Education is free to those who want to attend school. Boys and girls can begin primary school at age 5. Many young children quit school to work. Pakistani high school ends at 10th grade. A few students go on to 11th and 12th grade to prepare for college.

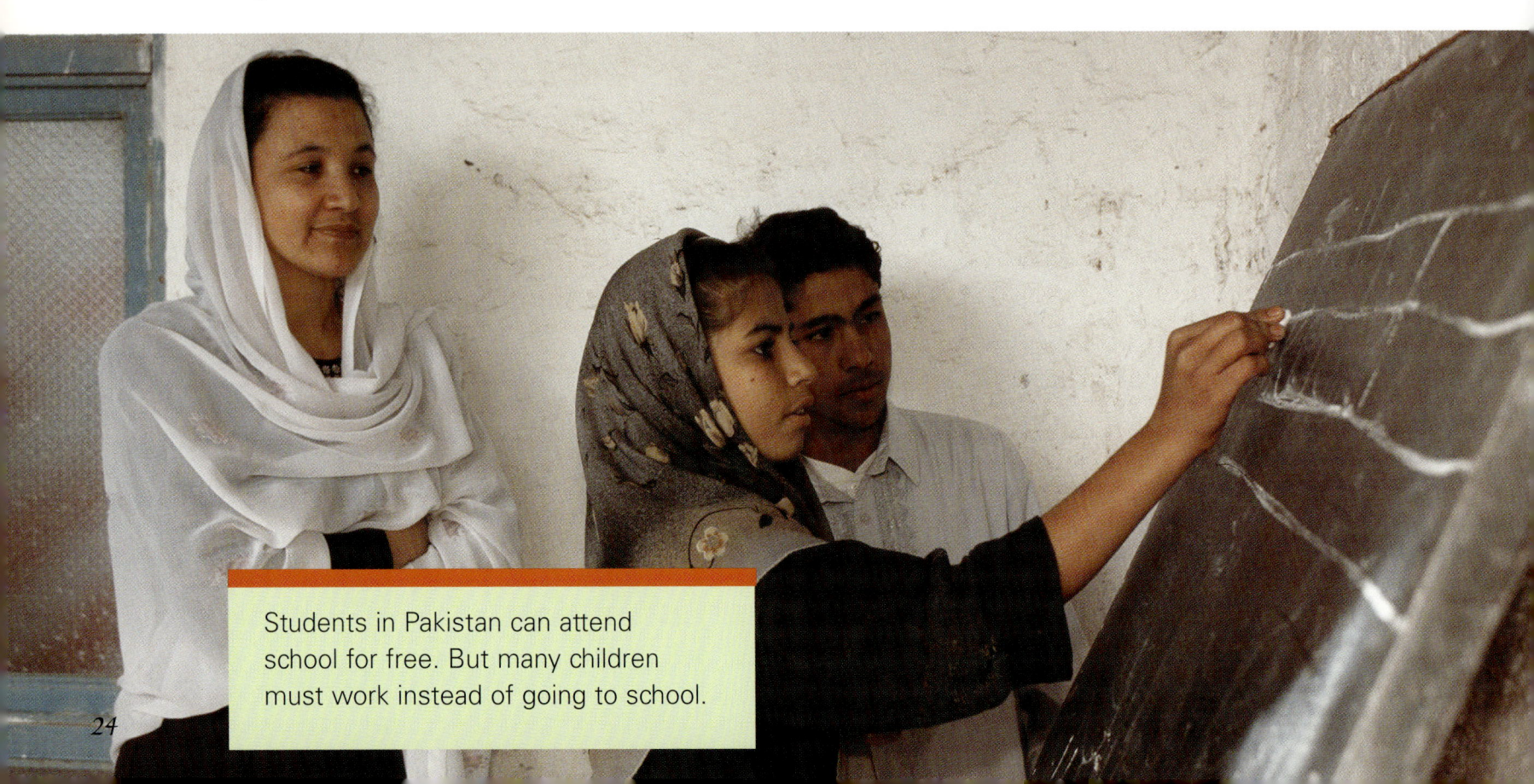

Students in Pakistan can attend school for free. But many children must work instead of going to school.

Pakistani Flag Mosaic

Pakistanis fly the country's flag from their homes. The flag colors are green and white. The color green represents Pakistan's Muslims. The color white stands for other religions practiced in Pakistan. The design is a crescent moon and star. The crescent moon stands for progress. The star stands for light and knowledge.

Mosaic tile designs are popular in Pakistan. People decorate mosques with colored tiles. Sometimes, the tiles make a pattern. Other times, the tiles form a picture.

You can make a mosaic design of the Pakistan flag. Use colored paper instead of tiles. It takes time to glue each piece into place. But the finished design is worth the work.

What You Need

one sheet of black construction paper
strips of ½-inch (1¼-centimeter) wide white and green construction paper
white or yellow colored pencil
ruler
scissors
glue

What You Do

1. On the black construction paper, use a ruler and colored pencil to draw a line about one-third of the way from the left side.
2. Use the colored pencil to draw a crescent moon and five-pointed star. These designs should be in the middle of the area to the right of the line you have drawn.
3. With scissors, cut squares from the white strips of paper. Glue the white squares inside the area to the left of the line you drew.
4. Glue white squares inside the crescent moon and star shape. Cut some of the squares into triangles to fit the moon and star shapes.
5. Cut squares from the green strips of paper. Glue them in all the areas around the white moon and star.
6. Cut some green squares into triangles to fit them around the crescent moon and star designs.

CHAPTER 7

Pets in Pakistan

In Pakistan, pets are more common in the city than in the country. Poor families in rural areas often cannot afford to keep pets. Farm homes are small and often crowded. Even so, farm families sometimes bring their cows or other animals in the house at night.

In Pakistani cities, families often have pets. Many people have dogs or cats. Some people keep chicks or rabbits as pets.

Birds are also popular pets in Pakistani cities. Many people own green parrots called "mithos." Others keep flocks of pet pigeons.

Some children in Pakistan may keep a lamb, goat, or other livestock animal as a pet. Most Pakistanis are too poor to own a cat or dog.

Pakistan's Sand Cat

The Sand Cat looks like a pet, but it is a wild animal. Sand Cats live in Pakistan's deserts. These animals are about the size of a small house cat. But unlike a pet cat, the Sand Cat can live without drinking water. The Sand Cat gets enough liquid from its prey.

Sand Cats hunt at night for food. They eat insects, birds, and rodents found in the desert. They can also hunt and catch snakes.

Sand Cats sleep during the day. They often dig shallow tunnels to protect themselves from the hot desert sun. They also find shelter under rocks and shrubs.

Sand Cats are night creatures. They look like pets but are wild animals.

CHAPTER 8

Sites to See in Pakistan

The most famous building in Pakistan is the Faisal Mosque. This religious building is located in Islamabad. Faisal Mosque is a large building that looks like a desert tent. Many believe it is the world's largest mosque.

Another famous site in Pakistan is the Badshahi Mosque in Lahore. This mosque was completed between 1673 and 1674. The tomb of Allama Iqbal is found at this mosque. He was a philosopher and poet. Iqbal was also a founding father of the country of Pakistan. Today, many visitors come to see this mosque.

Faisal Mosque is one of the world's largest mosques.

Badshahi Mosque in Lahore is a favorite place for people to visit and pray.

Words to Know

crescent (KRES-sent)—a curved shape; the moon looks like a crescent when it is a sliver in the sky.

fasting (FAST-ing)—giving up eating for a time

Islam (ISS-luhm)—the religion of Muslims, based on the teachings of the prophet Muhammad

mosaic (moh-ZAY-ik)—a pattern or picture made up of small pieces of colored stone, tile, or glass

mosque (MOSK)—a building used by Muslims for worship

Muslim (MUHZ-luhm)—a person who follows the religion of Islam; Islam is based on the teachings of Muhammad.

prey (PRAY)—an animal that is hunted by another animal for food

textile (TEK-stile)—a fabric or cloth that has been woven or knitted

To Learn More

Britton, Tamara L. *Pakistan*. The Countries. Edina, Minn.: Abdo, 2002.

Deady, Kathleen W. *Pakistan*. Countries of the World. Mankato, Minn.: Bridgestone Books, 2001.

Marx, David F. *Ramadan*. Rookie Read-About Holidays. New York: Children's Press, 2002.

Wood, Angela. *Muslim Mosque*. Places of Worship. Milwaukee: Gareth Stevens, 2000.

Useful Addresses

Consulate General of Pakistan, New York
12 East 65th Street
New York, NY 10021

Consulate General of Pakistan, Toronto
5734 Yonge Street, Suite 600
Toronto, ON M2M 4E7
Canada

Embassy of the Islamic Republic of Pakistan
2315 Massachusetts Avenue NW
Washington, DC 20008

Pakistan Cultural Society of Sudbury
961 Auger Street
Sudbury, ON P3A 4A7
Canada

Internet Sites

Do you want to find out more about Pakistan?
Let FactHound, our fact-finding hound dog, do the research for you.

Here's how:

1) Visit *http://www.facthound.com*
2) Type in the **Book ID** number: 0736821694
3) Click on **FETCH IT.**

FactHound will fetch Internet sites picked by our editors just for you!

Index

Afghanistan, 6
artists, 10

Badshahi Mosque. See mosque
Baluchistan, 6
birthday. See celebration

celebration, 21, 24
children, 8, 12, 15, 20, 21, 24, 26
crafters, 12
crops, 5, 6, 14

desert, 16, 27, 28

Eid-al-Fitr. See celebration

factories, 6, 12, 20
Faisal Mosque. See mosque
family, 8, 20, 26
farmers, 12, 13, 14
flag, 23, 25
food, 6, 19, 21, 22

herders, 12, 14
housing, 12, 14, 20, 26

India, 8, 10
Indus River, 18
Iqbal, Allama, 28
Islam. See religion
Islamabad, 5, 28

K2, 4, 5

Lahore, 28, 29
languages, 5
legend, 8, 9, 10–11
livestock, 14, 26

money, 5, 23
Montgomery, T. G., 4
mosaic, 25
mosque, 22, 25, 28, 29
mountains, 4, 6, 17
Muslim. See religion

North-West Frontier Province, 6

pets, 26, 27
population, 5, 6
pottery, 10, 11, 12
Punjab, 6

Ramadan. See celebration
religion, 5, 22, 23, 24, 25

Sand Cat, 27
school, 15, 24
seasons, 16, 18
Sindh, 6

transportation, 6, 14, 16

32